Twitter

(A Little Birdie Told Me)

Building your business
one tweet at a time

Henry J. Button

The Butler Publishing Group

ISBN-10: 1442174269
ISBN-13: 9781442174269

Printed in the United States of America.

Contents

1

Introduction to Twitter

Take yourself to the Twitter website and you might wonder what all of the fuss is about, or how the service could possibly be of any use to the business community. After all, Twitter tells us that they allow people to answer the question, "What are you doing right now?" At first glance Twitter seems almost to be a banal invitation for streams of people to broadcast constantly about their cats and socks. Some do use it that way. Yet businesses have discovered a whole host of opportunities through Twitter.

There are not many really useful business tools that can lay claim to being 100% free. Twitter does, however, and while the opportunities it presents aren't really obvious at first glance, they're still manifold. Business users are learning new ways to turn Twitter to their advantage each and every day. Surprisingly, one of the best uses of Twitter is to add some human personality to you, your brand, and your company. One of the worst uses? Posting links to your own websites, day after day after day.

Many of Twitter's users are organizations and events, not

individual people, so you'll be in excellent company when you turn to Twitter for your business. With 6 million users and counting, however, you cannot afford to miss out, whether you're a multi-million dollar corporation or a small one-man outfit working out of your garage.

Twitter Myths and Misconceptions

There's a lot of buzz about Twitter, ironic enough for a buzz creation tool. There are some myths, misconceptions, and negative perceptions of Twitter that should be addressed before you go leaping into the waters. Let's take a look at a few of them.

Twitter is a big waste of time where nothing valuable is said. Twitter is certainly a place where people are more than capable of putting together a stream of inane chatter, but this sort of use has dried up. The focus for many people is staying in touch with brief bytes as well as sharing links, information, and events. Businesses use Twitter for brand management, pre-selling, relationship building, public relations, customer service and tech support. You are also able to manage what you see by simply choosing not to follow anybody who fails to be of regular interest to you.

I can't track my ROI on Twitter. This is true—and then again it isn't. There are programs out there which will help you track the effectiveness of your Twitter posts. You can also track the amount of traffic that goes to your other websites from Twitter. Unless you are talking about the ROI on your or your employee's time, there's really not even an "I" in the ROI—because Twitter's free, as are nearly all of the applications that go with it.

Introduction to Twitter

Nothing useful can be said in 140 characters. Again, here you'd be wrong. Not only can links easily be shared in 140 characters, but you can also share small tips. For those who use Twitter to broadcast from conferences or seminars in real time, the notes they take can also be taken in 140 character bursts. You just can't do a deep, involved, long running blog post in 140 characters. Twitter will let you link to that deep, involved, long running blog post instead.

I'll never be able to keep up. You do not have to follow everyone who follows you—especially if you're a business. You should only follow people who you find useful and valuable. Unlike other social media people don't waste a whole lot of time getting their feelings hurt if you don't feel like following them in reciprocal fashion—again, particularly if you're a business. In addition, most people don't bother reading tweets once they scroll off the page.

I'll have to build up thousands of followers for Twitter to be worth my while. This is simply not true. You just need enough followers in your target market to be effective—rather like any other sort of web traffic. You should also be aware that due to the nature of "retweets" Twitter can act virally whether you gain new followers from it or not.

The Mechanics of Twitter

You get exactly 140 characters to make a post through Twitter. Wondering what you can do with 140 characters? The same thing that writers of billboard slogans have been doing for decades to capture the attention of people speeding down the highway at 75 miles per hour. People have a similar attention span on the internet unless something captures their attention—inspires them to pull over. As a

Twitter (A Little Birdie Told Me)

business person, Twitter is your opportunity to run a sort of streaming billboard to a group of dedicated followers.

You of course also have the opportunity to follow others, and this can be a huge benefit to you. You can follow your customers and find out what they've got to say. You can follow potential business partners. You can follow other industry leaders in a way that helps you stay current. You can monitor your competition. You can even do searches to see what people are saying about you.

Some people have described Twitter as "microblogging," but in truth this description is just a little bit inaccurate. Twitter really has very little in common with a blog at all. However, Twitter works wonderfully in concert with your blog by allowing you to "tweet" out an enticing headline that might encourage one of your followers to go read what you have to say. You can use this technique to drive traffic to a marketing event, opt-in e-mail list squeeze page, on-line press release or new product launch webpage, as well. Twitter works best in concert with other web pages.

Because Twitter works so well as a vehicle to get people to your web pages (though not exclusively—you've got to send people to other useful things or you're going to come across as a spammer), a "Twit This" button is one of the most useful things you can place on each page. Visit http://twitthis.com/ for URLs and plug-ins you can use to encourage other people to Twit your web pages (which is always going to be more effective for you than you Twitting your own).

For the busy professional Twitter offers yet another benefit —the ability to interact with the service through your mo-bile phone. By sending a text message to 40404, you can tweet no matter where you are. You can also pick up the tweets you are watching in this fashion. Twitter also offers the Twitter IM and twitter@twitter.com as platforms for getting your tweets out. In fact, Twitter is the only social network that does not rely on the web alone to get its messages out. This ability is part of what makes Twitter so unique—and so important to emerging marketing trends.

Twitter is a very useful brand management tool, which means it's important to pay attention to what you are doing from the moment you set up your account. For example you need to use your name, or the name of your business, not a nickname. You need to use your logo, or your personal photograph, and not an icon with a dancing strawberry on it unless your logo happens to be a dancing strawberry.

You only have 160 characters to spend on your bio. This will force you to be short, sweet, and concise, but do not skip this step. This is the time to let people know what you or your company is all about. People will check out the profile. If you find it difficult to craft such a thing in only 160 words consider this your crash course in learning how to effectively tweet!

As you fix up your profile you'll also have the opportunity to set a background. You can either create your own or use a template. Creating your own is best for branding purposes. If you don't have access to a professional template designer you can use http://freetwitterdesigner.com/ to put something together that's your own, or even use Power Point. Instructions on using Power Point to create a unique Twitter background are available at http://theclosetentrepreneur.com/create-a-twitter-background-using-powerpoint.

At first you're not going to have any followers—but that's okay. Your starting point is finding people to follow by searching interest groups in the search box. Go ahead and find 30-40 interesting people to follow. A surprising number of them will turn around and follow you, too. In addition you should do a search for anyone already talking about your company, product, or service. These are people you should be following to begin with. Go ahead and read what's being said, getting a feel for twitters and tweeting. It will help you craft your own tweets later.

One great tool for performing interest searches is Twellow. Twellow, available at http://www.twellow.com/, categorizes people by interest, sort of like a Yellow Pages for Twitter. If you're looking for people in your industry or people who are served by your industry, Twellow is one of the easiest places you can start. When you begin following these people you'll get insights into their world that you never had before—and you will get your first set of followers.

Sometimes keeping up with all of these tweets can be a little bit overwhelming, which is why you might want to go ahead and get yourself a Twitter client right off the bat. One of the most popular clients is Twhirl, available at http://www.twhirl.org/. Twhirl will help you shorten long URLs (very useful when some of the URLs you might want to share could potentially push the limits of every one of those 140 characters). It also greatly enhances your ability to perform the searches which are so important.

You may have noticed "Follow me on Twitter" buttons on other people's web pages or social networking sites. It's a good idea to add this to your own business web page as well, so that people who are already interested in your business can go right ahead and get linked up. It's also true that success tends to breed success—the more followers you can generate for your Twitter account the more followers you'll receive and the more dividends you will reap. Using a "Follow me on Twitter" link can also increase your SEO, which means more traffic for you as your Google rankings increase.

Twitter will also help you maintain a professional edge by providing a forum where you can get fast answers to questions, new knowledge and links you wouldn't have found on your own, and potential solutions to problems. There is not a business person alive who does not eventually need the services of some manner of vendor. Twitter can help you find those vendors and forge a relationship with them. Useful URLs from other people can help you stay on top of the cutting edge without spending hours reading through trade magazines. Others will show you what they've found to be important and if you're in luck that day you'll find it to be important, interesting, or useful as well. It's Web 2.0 at its finest—users reaching out to one another to carve meaning out of the massive sea of the World Wide Web. And on the Web, the only true measure of meaning is finding those pages or content which are helpful to you.

Getting Started as a Tweeter

What do people love to see tweeted? The same things they love to see anywhere else on the Internet. Value! You can provide value with links, not just to your own blog posts or web pages, but to other useful blog posts or web pages. You can add statistics, news headlines (with links to the article), or anything else that lets you build relationships through this powerful social networking tool. If you've ever sent a colleague something for no other reason than you thought it would be of interest to him, then you've already got a good handle on tweeting even if you didn't know it.

As you begin to tweet you might notice that some people begin to send you private messages. Always make sure you return the message in kind, even if it's only a brief acknowledgement. This is just polite. It also helps you continue to grow relationships with those who follow you.

Another great thing to do with your Twitter account is using it to ask questions. Asking questions can help you get a pulse on the market. It can help you gather content and ideas for your other web pages. It can help you interact with the community at large, spark dialogue, and generate buzz. You never have to directly sell on Twitter—nor should you—but Twitter is a very effective pre-selling tool.

If you have employees, your employees can all use business Twitter accounts too. This is especially effective out of the sales and public relations department. You should not discourage them from posting a personal note or two either—one of Twitter's great strengths is that it allows your public to see you, your business, and your employees as actual human beings.

Another cutting edge use of Twitter is as a medium for customer support. A support desk account for your company can allow quick, simple answers to customer questions in a way that is far more personable than leaving your customers hanging in a phone cue. Comcast, for example, has done this to great effect, and more and more companies are following suit.

You do need to take note: you can't edit your tweet once you submit it. Be very sure the tweet you put out there is the tweet you want the public to read.

Another skill you'll want to master is the art of the retweet. When you retweet, you take someone else's tweet and broadcast it to your followers, launching the message with the initials "RT" to start. As a business person your initial reaction may be to ask why you would possibly want to give this kind of boost to your competition. Just remember that you're building value and showing yourself to be a member of the community, so the benefits can actually be greater for you than for the original tweeter. In the upside-down world of internet relationship building caring and sharing is king. It may sound silly, but when you market on the internet you have to focus on the "kinder, gentler, more human" segment of the business equation in order to succeed. You should always credit the original poster by putting @postername behind the RT. Then you can add the content to your tweet.

@Signs and #Hashtags

You can post a reply directly to another user by starting your message off with the @username command. This is not a direct message so much as it's a reply to a specific tweet. Anyone can see an @reply, whereas a private message is private. A private direct message can only be sent to someone you follow, but an @reply can be attached to any post.

Do not underestimate the immense importance of @replies. The strength of Twitter is your ability to have a conversation with customers, prospects, and like-minded people. This is an absolute must for doing business on Twitter—asking questions, and responding to other people's questions. Think of Twitter as an amazing, massive cocktail party. You already know how to forge connections and relationships at a party: Twitter is much the same thing. Twitter demands two way relationship building—even with the billboard metaphor you will do yourself a disservice if you don't join the discussion and conversation.

Adding a hashtag, or #tag, to your post allows you to categorize it. Creating topics in this fashion can help people who are interested in a discussion you're hosting find you. Because others have done the same you can find those who are going to be advantageous to you. #tags are especially great for promoting new products, getting meeting notes up around the world in real time, and finding hot trends for market research. #tags make it easy to find your topics in a search, but adding #tags to every post makes them less useful, so use them with care.

You can place a #tag at any point in the Tweet to make it work, whether at the beginning, end, or middle of the text. A quick tweet to explain what your #tag is about will avoid some confusion as the #tag might not be quite as obvious to other people as it is to you.

Useful Twitter Services

The Twitter webpage itself is a little inefficient, which is why people tend to use clients and cell phones to interact with it more than they use the site itself. Twitter, on its own, also does not provide all of the services you might want to use it for.

Bubble Tweet: (www.bubbletweet.com) will allow you to add video to your Twitter page. For business people who have embraced the power of viral video, You Tube, and multi-media, Bubble Tweet is an awesome application.

ChirpCity: (http://chirpcity.com/) If your business is of an exceptionally local nature then you'll immediately want to hook up with ChirpCity, which lets you find other users and posts in your city. There's a top cities list for an easy scan, or you can just enter your city into the search box at the top of the page. Not only will you be able to find people in your city who are active Twitter users, but you will even be able to hook up with local news feeds—very useful if your business is at all news dependent.

#Hashtags: (http://hashtags.org/) This site will let you search for #tagged items as well as tracking the tags that have been recently discussed. This is useful either for deciding what the hot topics are or in searching out topics that are relevant to you and your business.

Matt: (http://www.themattinator.com/) Matt stands for "Multi-Account Twitter Tweeting." If you run multiple lines of business or websites and have a Twitter account for each one because each one targets a different audience, then Matt is for you. It allows you to post to multiple Twitter accounts without having to log on to each one of them.

StockTwits: (http://stocktwits.com/) If you are in any kind of investment business StockTwits may be a great tool for you. It allows you to focus on following and talking with investors and traders who are talking about news and conditions on the market.

TwitterCal: (http://twittercal.com/) This helps you combine two functions, your Twitter account and your Google Calendar. If you use your Google Calendar often in order to stay organized then you might find the ability to Twit events straight to your calendar to be more than a little useful.

Twitter Counter: (http://twittercounter.com/) This is a widget that you can add to a website. It will track the number of followers you've gained over certain periods of time and predict your future follower numbers based on the current activity. Business users will find this invaluable for tweaking their Twitter campaigns.

TwitterHawk: (http://www.twitterhawk.com/) Twitter-Hawk finds people talking about a chosen topic and then automatically sends someone a message if they Twit about it. For example if you sell jackets in a certain city and someone in that city Twits about jackets, TwitterHawk will automatically send them a message from your account. Some people consider this to be a form of spamming, so be wary. Others consider it to be a form of targeted marketing. You be the judge.

TwitPic: (http://twitpic.com) Want to Tweet pictures? You can with an application known as Twitpic. The moment you put a Twitter account together you actually have a Twitpic account. You can use your phone, the site, or API. Using API, you go to http://twitpic.com/api/uploadAndPost to both post a picture and send an update to Twitter that you've posted new photos.

TwitteRel: (http://www.twitterel.com/) TwitteRel makes searching for other users by keyword simple—a factor that will be very useful to you especially in the early phases of using the service. It can be useful in the ongoing phases of using the service, too, as you keep track of the people who are talking about you.

Twittertise: (http://twittertise.com/) This is an awesome tool for anyone who is dealing with their company's marketing efforts, because it allows you to track the effectiveness of advertisements and posts you send out on Twitter. You can schedule posts by date and time, and edit or delete posts before they go out. Visit the site for a nice video explanation, but marketers will instantly understand the value of these analytics.

Twitzer: (http://shorttext.com/twitzer.aspx) Twitzer only works with Firefox, but if you just can't say it in 140 characters Twitzer's the site to visit. It will allow you to post longer tweets. It also converts Tiny Url (shortened links) back into normal links if you're having trouble figuring out what links to click on. The tweet will still show up to Twitter as 140 characters—users can "De-Twitzer" the text to have it pop up in its full form.

Xpenser: (http://xpenser.com/) Xpenser will let you use Twitter to track your expenses. You can use your iPhone, your e-mail, your SMS, voice posts, Twitter, IM, and more to get every expense tracked. You can also manage, analyze, and export your expenses elsewhere. Tax tracking is easier because you don't have to go through mountains of receipts. Large companies can use it to auto-file expense reports in real time.

Managing Your Twitter Time

Twitter, however useful a tool it can be for business, can be a massive time eater. You don't want to waste your time on Twitter at the expense of your other business activities —you want to use it quickly and efficiently to achieve what you want to achieve with it.

Having a plan for exactly what you want to do with your Twitter activity and why is the number one step you can take to make sure you don't while away the day posting and reading update after update after update. Everyone will tell you that you need an overall plan and strategy, but you should also have a strategy for that day's tweeting before you ever log on.

For example, Mondays might be devoted to managing your brand and PR, so you know that you'll spend Monday's Twitter time doing searches for things being said about your company and responding to them, then adding one tweet that directs attention to something about your company you want people to see. Perhaps you have your company involved in a community or volunteer effort that you want people's attention on, so you do a brief tweet about that which directs attention to the news article or calls for donations to the organization.

Tuesdays might then be devoted to building value by sharing industry links, publications, or tips. So you know on Tuesday you're going to do a little reading to find these things, or perhaps retweet something someone else tweeted in order to help them build their own brand and following (thus increasing your value and loyalty).

Wednesday might be devoted to showing the human side of the equation—just some sort of little random posts and some replies. Though it's difficult to quantify what these sorts of posts do for you experience has shown that they are important and should not be ignored.

The next skill you'll want to master is scheduling your Twitter time. Whether you devote a half-hour block of time to your Twitter marketing or spread it out over 3 ten minute intervals in the day, you need to make sure that you're spending just the necessary amount of time on your Tweeting and no more. Services that help you time-post your tweets are especially helpful to the business person for this reason—a quick half hour in the morning scheduling some useful tweets and then reading a few more, and then you can be back to other, equally important marketing efforts. Whether all of your marketing takes place on the internet or you have other factors to attend to, you know that running a successful business takes a lot of moving parts. Even if scheduled tweets sounds a little artificial to you, your audience will not know the difference.

Master the art of skimming. There is going to be a lot of content that flies by on Twitter that is simply not interesting or productive for you to interact with. Having all of this noise chirp to your mobile phone on a daily basis is going to get maddening quickly. A quick scan of the feed on your Twitter Client or on the web, however, will allow you to pick out what's of interest to you and make use of what holds your attention while ignoring stuff about the sandwiches people are eating.

Don't mass-follow other Twitter users. Not only does this increase the amount of noise you have to sort through, it also is a favorite technique of spammers. The fact is you do not have to follow every single person who follows you. You should follow people who are of interest to you and don't worry about following anybody else. Following is not the best way to develop followers in the first place. That said you should find some followers as the ability to get your message out on Twitter is still only half of the usefulness equation. Having access to other people's knowledge, skills, and found items of interest is equally valuable.

Be wary of following Twitter on your mobile phone as well. While texting a tweet to Twitter while waiting for lunch to arrive is not going to destroy your work productivity, having tweets ring constantly to your phone is. Our days are already rife with interruptions that can cause a negative impact on our ability to stay productive and focused—don't add another.

Potential Accounts to Follow

Since you are just getting started on Twitter you may still be floundering about who it might be useful for you to follow, particularly if you are not having much luck with your search terms. Here are a couple of solid business-centered Twits who might be of use to you.

B2BOnlineMktg: This Twit is chock full of interesting links and posts for anybody who is dealing both with a B2B business and Internet Marketing. There is not a frivolous tweet to be found.

BWBX: The business exchange. From their own bio: "BusinessWeek's Business Exchange users create business topics, collaboratively edit and aggregate content from the web and share with their network and others."

DellSmallBiz: As an outstanding example of how large companies have embraced Twitter, Dell Small Biz has advice on how to start, manage, and grow your business. Again, this is another one where every single tweet has something substantial to sink your teeth into.

sbbuzz: From their own bio: "Encouraging dialogue between small business owners, techies, social media mavens and the folks who love them. Host #sbbuzz chats every Tues. 8-10 PM EST."

home_business: Whether you work out of your home or not this Twit has some marvelous resources coming through the tweets daily. If you do work out of your home you'll find this one an even more valuable resource.

msnbc_business: MSNBC's business news posts and links throughout the day. This is particularly useful if your business needs to stay right on top of emerging business trends.

Reuters_Biz: This is the news feed from Reuters Business News. Again, if your business is very dependent upon the current news and events you'll want to go ahead and follow this one.

tradeshownews: Looking for tradeshows to attend? Tradeshow news will keep you up to date on what's available. Perfect if your prospecting methods are heavily tilted towards trade shows.

Just Do It

Most people just don't "get" Twitter when they get started, even after reading some explanations. That's okay. Twitter is one of those mediums where it is often better to try it out for yourself. Even if you get off to a slow start the key is to just jump in and get involved. Remember that you're not trying to answer the question of "what you are doing," but are instead turning your Twitting to a particular purpose. Once you've outlined that purpose for yourself you can begin to do well with the medium.

Even though you can never erase what you say on Twitter, however, you can always build back followers if you make mistakes and bore some initially. You should become good at twitting quickly if you pay attention to what captures your interest and what you like to see. What causes you to follow or dump someone? There's a high degree of likelihood that your own followers are reacting to very similar stimuli.

There's no need to get intimidated, because getting involved with Twitter, while requiring some degree of thought and strategy, really isn't rocket science. The same principles that have guided every other form of Internet marketing guide Twitter: stay valuable, stay interesting, and stay interactive.

How Business Has Embraced Twitter

Now that you've gotten a brief overview of the basics of Twitter, it's time to delve a bit further on how business has embraced Twitter. With NPR, the White House, and Carnival Cruises all making use of this social networking tool, it's clear that, however strange a medium it may be, Twitter has taken the business world by storm. Examining the way that other businesses have made Twitter their own will help you make the most of your own efforts.

Businesses Who Twit (And What They Are Doing)

This is by no means a comprehensive list—www.twibs.com, the Twitter business directory, lists at this time 12,770 businesses both large and small. Yet as you start to craft your own Twitter strategy it might help to know how some major corporations are making Twitter part of their business routine and what they're doing to make it work for them.

How Business Has Embraced Twitter

Baskin-Robbins: Between product advertisements and offering a daily trivia contest, Baskin-Robbin's tweets are a load of fun. Their contests, of course, are the way they stop and add value to the consumer. After all, all they're giving away is a soft serve cone—and a mess of goodwill. If your business has something small like this that you can give away then you might want to look into the BR model.

This is clever because Baskin-Robbins markets ice cream direct to consumers. Attempting to inundate them with industry news, customer service, or interesting blog posts just doesn't make a whole lot of sense. So BR kept their Twitter strategy right to the core of who they are—and it's working. 5,342 people follow Baskin-Robbins.

Comcast: Comcast twits primarily to deal with customer service issues, using their Twitter ID comcastcares. Different agents post within the blog to handle customer questions, concerns, and ideas. Comcast's tweets also serve the dual function of allowing them to find out exactly what's on customer's minds. Customers won't always write an e-mail or formal letter to address their ideas, and they certainly won't wait on hold for 56 minutes. With Twitter, customers can make themselves heard quickly and efficiently.

Over 13,000 users are currently following Comcastcares, and it's a sure bet that represents 13,000 customers who are still actively engaged with using the service. With television service becoming more and more competitive—especially as customer service jobs get shipped overseas, the Comcast customer service strategy is worth investigating.

Dell: Dell has a storm of Twitter accounts. One is for the Dell Outlet, which has "exclusive Twitter discounts and news directly from the Dell outlet." Another is just "Direct2Dell", which is headlines about Dell products, services, and customers. Alienware handles high-performance gaming PC news, products, and updates. IdeaStorm takes suggestions. They have Twitter accounts for different company functions and different parts of the world, 33 accounts in all.

Dell estimates that these sale alerts have generated $3 million in revenue, pretty impressive during a time of recession where computer companies are doing mass layoffs. Dell is living proof that trying to twit some special offers and deals not available anywhere else can be an invaluable way for any good or service to win new business via social networking.

GM: GM's Twitter account, GMblogs, seems primarily to be a tool for public relations. Given the storm of controversy over the GM restructuring and bankruptcy in 2009 it's not surprising that they would have opened up a department specifically for the purpose of twitting in response to worldwide comments about their work and attempting to answer in reply.

GM is making full use of the search function to bring up when someone is talking about GM in order to immediately respond with answers to questions or talking points. Some people have remarked on this as a waste of money for the corporate giant, and others feel the way they're doing it is distinctively Big Brother and creepy. They've also added some simple announcements, such as "RT @Steve-Fecht: RT @JFM_Photo: http://twitpic.com/5fecx - GM Vice Chairman Bob Lutz confirms Monday morning that the Volt is on schedule," which is perhaps a more productive use of their PR time. Your own PR attempts might not run so well on direct, unsolicited answers to company gripes, but instead on indirect answers to the issues those gripes raise.

How Business Has Embraced Twitter

H&R Block: H&R Block is another example of a company using Twitter for customer service, though their tone is a lot more toned towards building relationships than is Comcast's. In addition H&R Block runs tax seminars every Tuesday and Thursday evening where people can get their tax questions answered in real time—thus providing massive value to the consumer who might follow them.

H&R Block also effectively uses Twitter as a sales tool because it looks for people who are griping about tax issues and difficulties. Thus they can connect with these consumers and help guide them into an H&R Block office, thereby increasing revenue. This is a great model for someone who wants to combine the different functions Twitter has to offer.

JetBlue: JetBlue monitors customer concerns, even little ones like, "I can't find a quiet place to make a phone call in this terminal," and responds proactively to them. This is half customer service and half simple engagement—but it has been used to correct ticket problems or deal with customer needs before. They, too, have a department pretty much devoted to Twitter, but the primary Tweeter is Morgan Johnston in Corporate Communications.

The blogosphere is pretty much unanimous that Johnston stands apart in part because he'll sit and have a real conversation with someone via Twitter—and will instantly apologize if someone gets weirded out by a sudden follow seconds after the airline is mentioned in a tweet. At times he will adjust as necessary, but the primary purpose of Jet Blue seems to be to respond to customers in a better, faster way. He considers his use of Twitter to be an "information booth" – (you can read the conversation and a funny story about Twittering William Shatner at http://www.jonathanfields.com/blog/jetblue-twitter-customer-service-or-to-spy/).

Twitter (A Little Birdie Told Me)

Kodak: One of the ways Kodak gives their tweets value and keeps in touch with customers is by posting cool photos taken with Kodak cameras. It's no secret that people love seeing interesting pictures over the internet, but this strategy aims directly at photography buffs who might be inspired by them and, of course, seek out new Kodak equipment.

Kodak has also done some contests through Twitter. It seems mostly to use Twitter as a brand management tool—any other uses for it appear to be almost incidental. An additional feed, KodakIDigPrint, focuses on digital printing, along with industry trends, technologies, products and success stories.

Zappos: Zappos Shoes encourages employees to twit about their workdays and what's going on in them as a way of humanizing the company as a whole. Zappos even has a Twitter manual for its company. Zappos, too, uses Twitter to monitor its brand, but its way of encouraging every single employee to get on is certainly unique. You see them Twitting about everything from the Sci-Fi channel to the new Mexican restaurant the employees are trying out.

Tony Hsieh, CEO of Zappos.com, seems to really adore Twitter on a personal level, which might explain his corporate-wide strategy. Zappos, however, is routinely cited as a company that is "getting Twitter right," so it is a strategy worth studying. Zappos abandons everything else in favor of forging relationships and having some fun.

How Business Has Embraced Twitter

A Closer Look at Twitter Exterior Business Functions

Brand Management: When using Twitter to manage or establish your brand you will need to have a clear feel for what your brand is. Are you fun? Speedy? Serious? Down home? Knowledgable? Cutting edge? Try to sum up your brand in just one or two words (brevity is the soul of Twitter). Then, as you begin writing posts, you can make sure your tone and your content matches the "brand word" that you've decided on.

Remember that your brand is not really about what you sell, but how you sell it. Anybody can sell a widget. Yawn. What separates the big widget sellers from the little guys is the big guys have successfully branded themselves in a way that appeals to a large segment of the population. Twitter is all about showing who you are. So if your brand is that you're the "fun widget guy", then you need to ask yourself this question about every tweet: Is it fun? Is it funny? Is it a little irreverent? Does this match who I want my company to be? If it doesn't, leave it off, even if it would otherwise be a good tweet.

Consumer Education: Sometimes you have a product or service whose benefits to the end user are not entirely clear at first glance. You know what your service will do for customers, but customers really just aren't sure because it's complicated. You can use Twitter to help customers become acquainted with what they need to know. Sometimes a customer is not even aware of a need until they've been properly educated on what's now out there. They need to be taught why they need to get involved and how they need to get involved.

You can use Twitter to run "Twebinars" which can serve as Q&A sessions, or simply tweet in order to introduce your industry and what you do through blog posts (both your own and other people's), news articles, and success stories of how other people or companies have used what you do to great effect.

Customer Service: As so many companies have shown Twitter is an excellent customer service tool. You have to be aware that Twitter can't replace phone or e-mail based customer service—but it can be an excellent supplemental method of helping your customers. By doing searches for discussions about you, you can find the customers who are tweeting disgruntled things about your company. Then you can send them an @message asking if you can help them, or an @message that quickly and concisely solves their problem.

For a small operation this is not really advisable. The huge outfits making use of this function for Twitter have a staff devoted to the customer service aspects and use multiple posters. Unless, of course, you only cater to a small number of customers, so that using Twitter in this fashion becomes manageable.

Humanization: Maybe you just want to defray resentment by making sure the people in the Twibosphere know that you and your employees are human too, rather than a faceless monolith that just doesn't care about others. Perhaps you just want to seem in-touch with your customers and available to the world at large.

If this is why you're taking your business to Twitter then it is okay to Tweet more or less like a casual user, but keep your company name somewhere in your profile or user name all the same. WidgeCorpBob can then post about his taco habit and still keep his name out in front of the company and the people at large. Because people buy from people they know and like, this is also known as "pre-selling," (though it could be argued that anything you do to provide your customer with value is a legitimate pre-sale).

Market Research: If you need to do a lot of research before you launch a new product line or promotion, Twitter is like one massive, unpaid focus group. Whether you passively read posts to get a feel for your demographic or put out a question that directly asks them what you think, this is an extremely valuable way to put social media to work for you.

You can also use Twitter to solicit product reviews and testimonials from an existing customer base, which in itself serves as a form of market research. If you have a product that just isn't doing very well, now is your chance to find out exactly what's going wrong and why it's just not performing.

Public Relations: A small business can be devastated by bad PR a lot quicker than a large business can, so monitoring and addressing customer gripes before they can become big problems just makes good sense. It also makes sense to put a likeable face on your company. Twitter can help you do both of these things.

A public relations campaign will focus on what you do for your community. It will also focus on what you're doing to address specific problems and concerns, as well as ways on which you intend to improve performance. If you've had a specific problem lately Twitter is a good place to start.

Sales, Deals, and Discounts: If you are offering Twitter-specific sales, deals, and discounts, you'll still provide value to the people following you. If you do this exclusively however, with no further interaction with the people around you, you are missing a lot of the value of Twitter.

That's where Baskin-Robbin's method is so smart, because they've made the sales, deals, and discounts part of the interaction. Dell has stayed interactive with customer questions and comments even as they've focused primarily on product announcements and sales.

Intra-Organizational Twitter

Some companies aren't using Twitter to reach out to other people—they're using Twitter to stay in touch with their employees. Sales forces communicate, CEOs bring things down the pike.

Coordinating Projects: Not all organizations exist in one building, or even in one city. If you decide to use Twitter as an intra-organizational tool sending status updates for various phases of a project could be an extremely productive tilt for you to address. Opening new stores, for example, usually involves multiple steps and departments— Twitter will give you the ability to get those status updates in real time.

Forging Teams: Companies don't always have an easy time with team building. Management can sometimes seem distant from employees, and employees don't always understand the reason behind management's decisions. With Twitter you'll be able to bridge some of these gaps and put together a dialogue in ways that was previously not available to any organization.

Handling Rumors: Just as misunderstandings between management and the workforce can start to destroy morale and productivity, rumors can crop up that do even more damage. Through Twitter you can address—and perhaps spot—misinformation quickly, getting a good explanation out to your people and putting an end to fearful talk.

How Business Has Embraced Twitter

Open Door Policy: It's sometimes very difficult for employees to address concerns, questions, and ideas that they have. This is especially true if the idea is somewhat off the top of the head and isn't quite right for a full meeting. Yet these brainstorms can become full, excellent ideas when they're allowed a solid forum to bounce around in.

You don't have to be exclusively in-organization or out-organization on Twitter. With Twitter you can also create "Twibes", which will allow people in your company to post only to the company as well as to Twitter at large. Visit www.twibes.com to find out more about how you can put Twibes to use for your company.

Twebinars

A Twebinar is a web based seminar handled on Twitter over real time. In order to host one you and your participants will need a webinar interface, and you'll need to use either Hashtags or Summarize to get the job done. The conversation takes place on Twitter, even if you're using Webinar software like Go To Meeting.

If you go to a seminar and post the notes over Twitter in real time this is also considered a form of "Twebinaring," allowing you to share the best parts and highlights of what you are learning with your entire company (and, sometimes, anybody else who may be watching or listening).

Avoiding the Creepy Factor

Some Twitter users have complained that they find it exceptionally creepy to see a company they've just mentioned in a Twit suddenly start following them or replying to them. This can cause a dilemma—you want to reach out and respond to your customers but you certainly don't want them left looking over their shoulders at you in paranoia. How can you walk the fine line?

One thing you can do is to respond immediately with apologies and explanations if someone does express upset at being followed. Stop following the user immediately and leave them alone. This shows that you're willing to change course if something isn't right and that your intent is ethical.

Second, you can put the fact that you are attempting to respond to people using your product or service right in your bio, so readers are aware that you're trying to serve customers better. You might even mention that you do like to watch for tweets about your product or service and keep your ear to the ground so that you can make your product or your company even better.

Having a personal picture instead of a logo comes in handy here—people like having a human face to interact with. Corporations, all too often, come across as faceless, uncaring monoliths. Twitter is your opportunity to reverse that trend and this opportunity cannot be wasted. If you have a team of people working the Twitter accounts make sure which person is posting is always transparent so that you don't come across as shady or stalker-like.

Twitter Hacked

One issue you should be aware of is that Twitter is remarkably easy to hack, and several celebrities and large companies have already felt the burn. Twitter hackers tend to like to post messages that could have enormous negative impact on you and your image. Though you can't change

How Business Has Embraced Twitter

Twitter's lousy security, you can at least take your own precautions.

First, you ought to choose a password 10-12 characters long with numbers as well as letters, and don't use anything obvious. Too many people use their usernames, birthdays, pet's names, and other obvious things which experienced hackers can blow through with a simple assault. Choose something that's not obvious and you'll reduce the likelihood that your account will get hacked.

Second, be very certain that when you post to Twitter you are posting to Twitter; phishing assaults have been known to happen. Not only can you end up with a big mess to clean up, but if you're using any sort of Twitter client you could be opening the door for the hackers to get to the rest of your information. As with anything where computers are a large part of the process, security concerns must stay paramount.

3

Social Strategies

Part of Twitter's power is how it can interact with other media. This is, in fact, a power that many forms of internet marketing now share, and an appropriate strategy is necessary to take full advantage of everything these media have to offer. Internet marketing, particularly where social networking is concerned, works best as a net—with multiple points of contact moving in web like lines in multiple directions.

In order to craft a strategy for your company you have to be aware of how each possibility works together and how you can use Twitter to bring the possibilities together into a cohesive whole. On the surface, Twitter looks like a dinky little application, at best a way to connect with customers on a personal level. When you get a little deeper, however, you find that you can dig in and use Twitter as the core of an entire online marketing strategy, if you employ just a little time and planning.

Social Strategies

Understanding Who Interacts With Twitter

Most Twitter users are between the ages of 35-45. The younger demographic is over at MySpace. There's some overlap between the two demographics over on Facebook. So understand unless your product markets specifically to 35-45 year olds or other businesses, you are not reaching every single segment of your market by interacting on Twitter. This is why, in fact, using Twitter for customer service cannot replace traditional customer service applications.

These 35-45 year olds are tech savvy. They're comfortable with the web and the possibilities the web has to offer. 63% of them are men, and surveys have pointed to the idea that many, many Twitter users hold liberal political views. Most Twitter users earn more than 60K a year—a fact that should make any business owner sit up and pay attention if no other fact about Twitter does. 6.1 million people are logging in from the United States alone.

Politics, science, technology, news, and work related items are of great interest to the bulk of Twitter users (we're ignoring, for the moment, the people who post about sandwiches and dog walking). This can help you get a better understanding of the "hooks" that you need to employ to get Twitter users to sit up and take notice of what you have to offer.

The typical Twitter user also maintains presence elsewhere—a blog, Facebook account, MySpace account, or personal web page. Just as you are trying to increase your presence through Twitter, most Twitter users are trying to increase theirs. Understanding this can help you work with Twitter users in a reciprocal way that benefits both parties, and ultimately forwards your own goals.

Twitter (A Little Birdie Told Me)

In fact, the fact that a typical Twitter user is so hyper-con-nected works out great for you. For example, take a Twit-ter user who also has a Facebook account. Twitter has 6.1 million users—Facebook has 79 million users. But market-ing on Facebook is a much, much more difficult proposi-tion due to the way the media is set up—you have to be on a person's Friend's list on Facebook to even get near them, and people do not Friend on Facebook the way they follow on Twitter. Your ability to get to the cross-section, howev-er, means that a particularly good tweet can reach out to a much broader audience on a viral level. The same is true as links get posted to blogs or incorporated into other peo-ple's e-mail marketing. It may not be the direct impact that is as important to you as the indirect.

Talking About Problems or Talking About Brands?

Unless you are a very rare case, most customers don't real-ly care about your brand. This may seem counter-intuitive given all the time you're going to be establishing your brand—but it shouldn't. Your brand is a marker whereby your customers can quickly understand where you stand in relation to specific problems that they have. You care about your brand, and should. Customers only care about how you can serve them. Few brands generate the sort of cult interest that makes everything about that brand seem inherently fascinating to those who embrace it.

So even as you build your brand you know that you need to be zeroing in on the problems your customer has and offer-ing solutions—and that when it comes to Tweeting those solutions can't always be about what your company has to offer. Given that there are better forums and platforms to really get into the meat and potatoes of these problems than Twitter, you can turn your Twitter strategy directly on getting your customers to those forums in a way that benefits them.

For example, if you are marketing a medical product that helps with a specific medical problem, you could host a sort of "share your story" segment on your website and get tweets out about each particular story. Even if each story never directly mentions your product your brand is known to be the people behind getting these stories out and read. You're providing a service—and talking about specific customer problems.

You don't just have to find value to get on Twitter and get things rolling. Sometimes what you need to do is create the value and get the people on Twitter over to it. Creating value is the whole trick to any business to begin with—social networking just calls upon you to do it in new, innovative ways.

Understanding Your Company Culture

In order to craft any sort of social media strategy you have to understand your own company culture—whether you're a larger operation or a one man band. To some extent you are going to be using Twitter to craft a lens for others to look through and see part of your company. What parts are you going to present? What parts do you want to keep hidden? What level of transparency are you comfortable with?

If you're doing your own Tweeting for your own company this sort of self-examination is important. If you're going to have multiple people within the same organization using Twitter on behalf of the organization, this self-examination is vital. You'll need to craft some sort of policy or manual that your people can follow in order to get the most out of the departments who are spending the most amount of time working with social media.

Knowing these things can also help you decide what other touchpoints you're going to weave in and out of Twitter. It may be appropriate for one company to be on MySpace where it would be a complete waste of time for another company. You need to understand yourself, your audience, who you benefit. When you think of your ideal customer you need to think of individuals—the types of individuals you'll be interacting with—and not raw demographic numbers wherever possible. This will set your tone, your style, your chosen mediums and your content. Twitter will then point the way to these points of contact.

This is where you begin to draft the strategy that you'll take with you onto the web. This is not just about how you'll use Twitter (customer service or PR or whatever else) but how you'll make the most of internet marketing as a whole. H&R Block's strategy is not Baskin-Robbin's strategy. Misunderstanding who you are and who you market to is going to make everything you do a lot less effective. Coming to this understanding should make the elements of internet marketing snap into place for you in a way that allows you to move forward and stay on top of your game.

Integration

Often when people think of content on the web they think of words and words alone. There's no doubt that words are a major part of content. It is words that interact with search engines. It is words that generally tell people whether to go or stay, whether to come back or find somewhere else to be. The words are important.

Social Strategies

Words, however, are not all there is to content. A well-done how-to video that addresses your customer's need is good content. An audio podcast that listeners can download and play on their Ipods as they go to work or clean their houses which features an interview with a leader in an industry that benefits from your product is good content. Pictures—of events, conferences, new products, people using product—is good content. Flash games, java, and interactive contests, arcade games, or RPGs are excellent content as well. Content is not so much about the information—though information is important—as it is about what keeps people coming back to see you again and again. It's also not about specific websites anymore, though of course you'd like to drive traffic to your website. In point of fact your primary company website, even if your storefront is there, is not the primary spot you need people going to anymore. It's about what keeps people coming back to you: your product, your brand, or you personally.

Make no mistake—that 140 character limit does not mean people have stopped wanting to see engaging content. That 140 character limit helps you drive people towards engaging content. The more engaging and valuable the content you send people to, the more people will take the time to follow you on Twitter and then click on those links. It's not important to send them directly to places where they can buy things from you—they can find such places on their own. It's important for them to remember that you sent them there. In some cases, it's important for them to remember that you provided the content. The sales benefit comes later. In social networking this indirect approach will work better than a straight up info-dump about your product each and every time. Many people go on to Twitter thinking it's a nice new distribution network for the same old messages. It's only after they've been there awhile that they discover the fallacy of this notion.

Twitter (A Little Birdie Told Me)

So crafting your Twitter strategy is as much about crafting the other things you plan to offer elsewhere as it is about deciding what to tweet and why. Understanding how to link Twitter to other media is key.

Blogs: The most obvious place to start on Twitter is with blogs—after all, it's a natural progression. Yet whether or not you want to bother with a blog really depends on what kind of company you are. Professional writers, bloggers, and tech people do really well with blogs. Larger companies don't do so well—the public just doesn't trust them, for one thing, and depending on your product may be bored to tears by them for another.

Blogs are not that effective for B2B customers to be sure, because B2B blogs are notoriously boring, ineffective, and without value. Blogs are a much more personal venue. People communicate ideas to others on blogs effectively—organizations don't do so well at it. Therefore a sole proprietorship or partnership might do great with the right kind of blog, but a bigger organization is wasting its time. Any tweeting to blog posts the larger organization does, especially if it's B2B, should be on other people's blog posts that solve problems common to the group in a helpful way. Just an "Oh by the way, you might find this useful" sort of shout out rather than a tweet that you just posted this nifty thing that everyone needs to see.

Forums: As an inherently social media, forums work well with Twitter. Forum posters tend to ask one another specific questions, soliciting specific answers from one another. If you've chosen to host your own forum your tweets could focus on other people's very interesting posts, replies, and queries.

Hosting your own forum has a world of other benefits as well. For one thing, people that get involved with your forum have a good reason to visit your site again and again and again. Sure, they're going for the community bonds they're forging there and not for you, but again that's really not the point. The point is you, as the person hosting this community, stay at the forefront of their mind each and every day.

Given the number of other marketers who turn to forums as a way to get their own name out, you can use Twitter to help keep your forum lively and active. Focusing on those marketers wherever they are useful means they know they get extra bang for their buck by using your forum over other people's forums. This sort of win-win, mutually beneficial scenario means extra coverage for both of you—a partnership effort of a sort that's vital to establishing any internet marketing strategy.

Interactives: Interactives don't have to all be fun and games. A mortgage lender or realtor who puts a "mortgage calculator" on their website has just offered a useful interactive to their audience. A security company who puts a keypad training module on the site has done the same thing. An interactive is anything people can play with and experience. Whether this is just a fun game, a cool contest promotion, or an act of consumer education is rather immaterial in terms of the content factor—it just has to be something that will engage the consumer and be valuable to him.

Interactives take a lot of forethought and a great deal of programming know-how, so if you don't have the know-how at your disposal you're obviously not going to indulge yourself in this strategy. If you do have the know-how, however, a little creativity can take you a long way. Tweet about updates or additions to your interactive, Tweet about the fact that it's there, Tweet when someone has used your interactive and found it interesting or fun enough to mention elsewhere.

Some companies make interactive their entire strategy. Game sites that sell advertisement, for example. Or free RPG sites that sell both advertisement and memberships that give more in-game benefits. Companies with that sort of strategy won't twit about the fact that they have interactive content—but they might twit about high scorers, big winners, and new features, quests, or games available on the site.

Photos: Photo content is tricky, because it's sometimes hard to estimate the true value of the content to the consumer. Bottom line? If the visitor likes the photo you've created some value. Kodak's photo strategy makes sense for Kodak. If you're running a travel business travel destination photos make sense for you. If you're selling computers tweeting a big Flicker picture of a computer is probably not going to do a whole lot for you unless the computer looks extremely impressive and cool.

If you think someone's going to find some value in your photos, tweet away. Even if you're mistaken about the interest level inherent in the photo these little tidbits of content can still have the effect of humanizing you to your audience, which remains a vital function of Twitter no matter what your primary strategic thrust is.

Podcasts: Whether or not you podcast should involve, largely, how often you think you'll have something useful to say. Some people podcast once a week, just as if they were running a radio show. Some do some sort of very useful six part, four part, seven part, or other part series. The extent and amount of podcasting you might do depends largely on your equipment, your desire, and your ability to put such a thing together in a way that is going to be compelling.

Tweeting out every time you put out a new podcast or podcast series isn't a bad idea so long as there are other things that you are tweeting. Podcasts used in this fashion should usually be a free-subscribe product because you're using them as a platform to keep your name out there. You should not charge for podcasts unless charging for audio broadcasts is your primary source of income.

Social Bookmarking: It used to be that Digg and Delicious were major tools for getting an online strategy into play—part of the whole "social bookmarking" phenomena that was taking the web by storm and beginning to define "Web 2.0." Now people are beginning to use Twitter as a primary source for social bookmarking, putting things they like into their favorites and effectively doing the same things bookmarking sites allowed them to do in an easier interface.

That said there are a growing number of social bookmarking applications for Twitter, a way of bookmarking the bookmarks, so to speak. These bear keeping an eye on, but for now their usefulness is unclear. If you find an application you think will skyrocket your business, by all means try it out, but for now it's simply important to understand where Twitter has landed in the bookmarking field. As an aside, the "Twit This" button is considered a social bookmark more often than not.

Squidoo: Squidoo is something of a quirky site, and whether or not you use it will depend on the tone you want to set for your company. It's somewhere between a web hub and a social bookmarking site all by itself, created by the founder of permission marketing, Seth Godin. Twitter is another iteration of the permission marketing phenomena (people are free to block and un-follow you at any time, after all) and there's no rule among the "Squids" that says you can't post up a "lens" (short overview webpage) about your site. If your business is more serious or larger this may serve as an inappropriate forum—you have to decide how the tone and delivery meets your business needs.

That said, Squidoo features applications that link right back to your Twitter account, and seems to have embraced Twitter as a phenomenon. You can use Twitter to post updates to your lenses or post new lenses that you've made. If you're creative you can post a wide variety of lenses on topics related, in whole or in part, to what you do, or you can stick to your primary company lens. It's all up to you and what you want to accomplish with the medium.

White Papers: Posting white papers on the internet has become more and more common for B2B users, and this is where B2B internet communication shines far above the blogosphere. These white papers are unabashed marketing tools that are nevertheless chock full of good, solid, interesting information. They are nearly always available for free.

Tweeting about an interesting white paper you've found or posted is going to be a potential winning strategy if you are the type of business that embraces or employs white papers at all. White papers are generally high-value items to begin with, so even if you're sending people to your own papers you're still likely to escape some of the "me me me" stigma that can come along with ringing your own bell too much.

You Tube: Do not underestimate the popularity or value of solid video content. You Tube videos are extremely popular, and because they can easily be embedded across other media they turn viral quickly. Visuals appeal to a wide audience, and if you can put together (or find) anything with solid video value then you should twit it.

How-tos, speeches, lectures, music videos of up and coming bands—the possibilities for video content are as endless as they are for any other sort of web content. Again you are limited only by your creativity and individual business strategy.

4

Using Twitter to Fuel Your Bottom Line

As a business person you understand the value of relationships, customer service, PR, and the like—but you also understand that the ultimate goal of such activities is to fuel profits. Helping your business grow and prosper is the primary goal of any marketing or outreach effort you attempt. So long as you keep the 80/20 rule firmly in mind—80% of what you talk about has to be about your customers and 20% can be about you—you can still do some direct damage in this area—as Dell so aptly demonstrated.

So now we'll turn our attention to the most effective way to sell on Twitter, remembering there are some people who are adamant that one should never, ever sell on Twitter. Some people will stop following you for the very attempt to sell—but that's okay. You are in business to make money and someone who gets offended by the occasional attempt by your business to make money was not someone who was going to spend money in the first place.

It's important to remember that the most important metric

Using Twitter to Fuel Your
Bottom Line

for your Twitter efforts is never going to be your follow numbers. Yes, you need followers to make it work, but sometimes people follow for a number of reasons, and not all of those reasons have a thing to do with what you're doing. The most important metrics, ultimately, are still going to be connected with the money Twitter makes for you.

There are some Twitter snobs who will tell you that you can't sell on Twitter. You can't, can't, can't. Listening to them is counter productive. You can sell over the phone, you can sell on the television, you can sell over the radio, you can sell in person, you can sell through e-mail, and you can sell through Twitter. What you can't do is be obnoxious about it.

This is why you spend so much time on Twitter getting people liking you, interested in you, and enjoying what you have to say—so that when it comes time to make some money you can do so. Whether your focus is new customers, new products, or customer retention you will find the "Twitterati" are not so adverse to the normal course of commerce as some would like you to believe, if you've taken the time to build the relationships first.

Sales, Product Announcements, and Deals

Making announcements about what's new and cool is a very effective way to put Twitter to work for you. For the most part you can assume that those who are going to visit your website have already done so, if only to get some kind of an idea of what you're about. There's no point Tweeting those things again and again—but you should tweet whenever you're doing something new.

Got a new product? Tweet it. Got a new service? Tweet it.

Twitter (A Little Birdie Told Me)

Figured out how to offer something that's faster, better, or addresses problems with previous models? Tweet that too. Tweet it in a way that encourages people to come and see, to come check it out. You can do this by making it about them: "I listened and made it faster--check it out here," is only 89 characters, leaving plenty of room for an URL. Get the word out and generate some buzz—there are people who will not be paying attention at any other spot than Twitter, so get them to your site and buying from Twitter. You can do this even if you've been primarily using Twitter for customer service—especially if you couch the sales announcement in customer service terms.

Of course, you might have a fairly stable product or service that just doesn't change much—and that's fine. Use Twitter to announce fire sales, holiday sales, clearance sales, or other kinds of sales you might run. Bonus points if you make these sales Twitter-exclusive—that is you can only learn about them on Twitter and only get to the sales site through Twitter. This not only saves you some money by limiting the amount of slashed prices you're offering around the web but fosters a sense that you are promoting loyalty in and to the Twitter community.

If you're offering any kind of deal or special the same applies—this is something new and different you're doing, and you'd be doing your community a disservice by failing to let them know about it. Again, you'll get bonus points with the Twitter crowd if the deal you offer is only available through the posted Twitter link. Yes, this takes a bit more web work on your part, setting up special pages or codes or what have you—but it builds the loyalty you've been working so hard to attain on your social media venture.

Making the sales and deals exclusive will also help ensure that people buy. People love to feel like they're part of an exclusive club offering exclusive benefits. If you're judicious about this and don't offer these sales all the time you'll ensure that people want to take advantage of a short term deal. People also love to feel like they've been smart and waited for the most advantageous time to buy. If you don't over-use the technique then you can find it a very nice way to spike profits and boost sales every now and then.

Just as further proof that selling on Twitter is not as taboo as folks would have you believe, check out http://www.tweetseller.com/, a website that specifically catalogues when people are trying to sell things on Twitter. Though these tweets read a little like person-to-Twitter garage sales or classified ads, the fact is that buying and selling are happening. If your business model previously relied on Ebay then you might find that Twitter is a faster, more effective way of getting the job done after all. Tweet-seller is not affiliated with Twitter, but it still pulls in sales related Tweets.

Affiliate Marketing Links—Good, Bad, and Ugly

Some people, of course, have one primary business online —they are professional affiliate marketers. Twitter can be a tricky, tricky playground for directly selling affiliate links —there's just something about them that really sends Twitter people into a—twizzy—when they spot them. So you have to tread carefully and understand what you're doing and why you're doing it.

Who Should Affiliate Market on Twitter: If you are an affiliate marketer who has focused exclusively on one type of product—i.e. books—then you do have a leg to stand on when it comes to affiliate marketing. You'll have some choices to make about how you do it but you can eas-

ily brand yourself as "that person who talks about books."
If you always make sure to promote only books that you
genuinely enjoy as part of a genuine conversation with
your followers and put in your bio that you'll be posting affiliate links to the good ones, then people won't follow you
unless they don't care about affiliate links and want to hear
about books. You should of course post about the bad
books as well—without an affiliate link. As people begin to
trust your recommendations you might find this very effective. This works better the more specialized you are—a
book lover who sticks specifically to one category, say,
mysteries, is going to do better than a book lover who posts
about every book under the sun.

Who Should Never Affiliate Market on Twitter: If
you're one of those affiliate marketers who gleefully (and
sometimes even effectively) makes your living marketing a
vast variety of products then Twitter is not a good forum
for directly slipping those links in more often than not.
This is because you're going to have a hard time distin-
guishing your brand. You're also going to have a hard time
keeping things very relevant. Now—you may be an excep-
tion to the rule, but in general...you should not be trying to
directly tweet your affiliate links if this is you. You can
choose one category to work with as a Twitter brand only if
you wish to move yourself into the first category.

You should also avoid affiliate marketing on Twitter if
you're in any other kind of business. Let's face it—a tax
professional stopping to affiliate market some software or
an e-book is going to be a bit jarring and strike people as
irrelevant and out of place. If you're in some other kind of
business any income you make on Twitter is going to be
completely incidental—not worth risking the hard work
you've already done branding yourself and gaining your
following.

Using Twitter to Fuel Your
Bottom Line

Who Can Sometimes Get Away with Affiliate Marketing on Twitter: Casual users who just chit chat on Twitter can sometimes get away with posting very relevant links to products they truly love, enjoy, own, and trust. This is more like a quick favor with a couple of bucks attached than a true marketing strategy, and followers will generally forgive 1 or 2 tweets stuck in the middle of a conversation if it makes sense to have them there.

Training your Own Affiliates: Perhaps you're not going to be doing the affiliate marketing yourself. Perhaps you are a businessperson who recruits affiliates to get your product sold, and quite a few of these individuals are on Twitter. Fair enough—but make sure you do it the right way. Recently the internet was abuzz about an internet marketer who provided imbedded affiliate link tweets. People were posting to get his book FREE all over Twitter —and when all those posts were lined up they looked a heck of a lot like spam. There was some backlash over this effort, and even the marketer stood up and admitted that people who stopped to personalize his message got way better results than the people who simply posted the canned one. You can read the full blog post about the faux pas here: http://www.problogger.net/archives/2008/10/08/affiliate-marketing-on-twitter-does-it-belong/.

Understanding the backlash you can cause against yourself and your own affiliates with a bad move, it's important for you to train your affiliates with a strategy that you are comfortable with and that does not make you (or them) appear to be spammers. You have to be really careful on Twitter, not just because you might lose some followers. Twitter itself is pretty harsh on people they consider to be spammers and will block accounts that seem to exist for no other reason than to push annoying marketing messages on their followers. You don't want to lose access to this lucrative forum—or have to start again from scratch.

Crafting a Strategy: Twitter users are divided on whether or not affiliate links belong on the site—but nobody is divided about the fact that users don't appreciate deception. Therefore you can't try to hide the fact that you're trying to slip an affiliate link in there. Some users recommend just putting a hashtag on the post that says #affiliatelink. People are free to follow your link, ignore your link, or Google the product themselves if they're really so adverse to buying from an affiliate.

Other users note that one of the strengths of affiliate marketing is the ability to post a balanced review, and suggest affiliate marketing only if you have a blog. This allows you to link to the product review blog post. You can then put your link into the post. In this fashion you're continuing to provide value while still having a venue for placing your links. This is without a doubt the least intrusive way to get your affiliate links to Twitter users, and is absolutely the safest if you wish to avoid making problems. You might wish to experiment to see if links in the tweets are more effective than links in blogs, but the long term benefits of avoiding backlash might outweigh a slightly higher conversion rate at the outset.

Again, affiliate marketers should only try to market products that they use and trust themselves. An affiliate marketer may be able to get away with marketing products they've never personally touched elsewhere on the web, but it's not going to fly on Twitter.

Above all, however, your followers expect you to keep your affiliate links, if any, relevant to the conversation and in line with your brand. Defy the expectations you've created at your own risk.

Using Twitter to Fuel Your
Bottom Line

Twitter Customer Retention Strategies

Finding new customers is always great for business. Finding new customers is how business grows. However, if you can't retain the old customers you find yourself starting from scratch again and again, each and every month. The key to a healthy business is getting the same customers to buy from you again and again and again.

Using Twitter to retain and reward customers is just good business. The customer service applications of Twitter are not the only forces at work here. You could use Twitter to thank customers, create a customer rewards program, or to spotlight customer efforts and stories. Any indirect post that helps you keep a customer will contribute to the health of your bottom line, providing a foundation for growth.

Twitter, of course, is not the be-all and end-all of customer retention. Yet nothing retains customers like building and growing relationships with them. Sometimes even pausing to talk to customers like a human being does the trick. We've long ago left the shores where people walked into neighborhood stores and chatted with their neighbor the shopkeeper. Through social networking, however, we can bring a 21st Century twist to a 1940s model.

Finding Customers at a Point of Need
(Lead Generation)

A great deal of Twitter "buzz" revolves around the way Twitter helps business owners find customers at their "point of need." This is where doing some focused Twitter searches can really help fuel your profits. People occasionally tweet about problems they're facing, questions they have, or needs they have to get addressed—but aren't sure how.

For example, let's say you're in the transportation business. A new farmer comes on Twitter and laments that they're expanding and not sure how to deal with the distribution logistics. Voila. A reply or direct message with some useful information or an offer to talk is right there with a hot customer who has a real and present problem that you can solve, and solve well. Even @replying with, "I do distribution, can I help?" Or, "I do distribution, do you want to bounce some ideas off me?" can open a dialogue with someone you might never have found otherwise.

This is where a lot of people miss the boat—people are spending more time tweeting than they are listening, and listening is really where twitter can begin to work for you at its most powerful. To truly take advantage of it in a strategic way you should make a list of keywords associated with your business and do a daily search as a part of your sales related activities (not your pure Twitter related activities). You're still doing this on Twitter, but the other things you've done on Twitter count as your Twitter activities. This is pure prospecting.

You do, however, have to avoid coming on too strong—and back off immediately if your "prospect" expresses discomfort with your interaction. In many cases, however, if someone has a need pressing enough to tweet on it they'll appreciate a solution presenting itself, particularly if that solution (you) presents itself in a polite, friendly way. Don't lead off with "sell sell sell," and you'll generally be fine.

Don't underestimate the value of free items when you're

trying to earn customers through meeting their needs. Remember that a favor done today builds loyalty tomorrow - and it may be that a little free piece of advice or whitepaper is really all that person needs today. You've done your job if you've gotten your name out and built tomorrow's relationship.

Techrigy offers a program called SM2 alerts that will go ahead and automate this search process for you and send you alerts when it picks up on a potential lead. Rather than taking the time to do the searches yourself the searches can be sent to your inbox so you can open up a dialogue. Each of these leads is warm, so you have a better chance of scheduling the phone call, setting up the appointment, or opening an e-mail dialogue to create new business. The extent to which you'll do this depends on your business size, but this method is especially effective for smaller businesses and highly effective for B2B users.

You can also send follow requests to these people so you can keep an eye on what they're doing and the way their needs evolve over time. If you're selling something that is not a one-time product or service but needs periodic meetings or updates, then this would be an ideal lead-generation strategy for you.

Remember to tweet about 3-6 times a day if you're serious about using Twitter as a lead generation tool. Different people are around at different times, and few scroll back to the last update they read. Most people skim the page that's up and then move on from there. Sure, you'll catch some people on their mobile phones (again, and again, and again) but you want to cast as wide a net as you possibly can.

ROI

Twitter (A Little Birdie Told Me)

When you start talking about the bottom line it's natural to want to try to quantify the successes Twitter is bringing to you. After all, you have a certain amount of time, energy, resources, and money to spread around, and you want to make sure you're making the most of each of them. Though some naysayers insist it's impossible to track anything better than "engagement" on Twitter, Dell's successes have proven that it's possible to track actual hard numbers about what's going on with your social networking efforts, numbers that go beyond who is following you.

Google Analytics: When you get Google Analytics working with Twitter you can use it to determine your conversion rates—and from there you can determine the actual income that Twitter has brought to you. You won't be able to measure everything this way, it's true—the method for getting Twitter to work with Google Analytics won't record anything that comes off a Twitter client, for example—but you'll still get some numbers to play with. Those numbers will give you some solid sales figures to evaluate.

The method for getting these two programs to play nicely with one another is just a little bit arcane, but you can find out how at: http://www.devwebpro.com/2009/02/27/how-have-google-analytics-recognize-twitter.

TwitterAnalyzer: TwitterAnalyzer is less about hard sales numbers and more about your quality time with Twitter. It measures things like the number of followers that are on at the same time you are on, the amount of retweets you're receiving (which is so much more a measure of exposure than straight followers), and even demographic information about your followers which can help you target your campaigns all the more.

Using Twitter to Fuel Your Bottom Line

True, these sorts of analytics are softer numbers—but they're soft numbers that can help you make adjustments and get more effective in a short amount of time. They're numbers worth looking at. They're numbers that grow, change, and shift into time, which translate into charts that you can hand out to the less tech-savvy members of your company. That will help them understand what exactly it is you're doing with this "Twitter thing."

Of course, all of these things have to be put in perspective versus the time that you're using on Twitter—which can be a harder number to measure, particularly if your Twitter efforts are intermittent or spread out through the day. If you've got an entire department devoted to Twitter than ROI becomes a lot more important—you have to factor in wages (or salary), insurance costs, and all the other costs associated with having a workforce doing anything at all in your organization.

5

Twitter Best Practices
and Strategies

All the mechanics in the world aren't going to help you if you can't make a good impression. Twitter is, after all, a medium for communication and socialization. Just as you can make a fool out of yourself at a cocktail party and blow a big business deal, you can really shoot yourself in the foot on Twitter by ignoring the written and unwritten rules.

First, you should make sure none of your strategies or behaviors emulate the known and detested behavior of Twitter-spammers. Twitter red flags the following "spam-like" behavior:

• Following a large number of people in a very short amount of time. (Spammers do this in the hopes that those people will turn around and follow them, thus allowing them to subject a large number of people to their marketing messages).

• Following and unfollowing people in a really short amount of time. Twitter especially watches for people who use bots to do this. Using bots on Twitter defeats the purpose of Twitter anyway—there's never any good reason to do it. Twitter also takes notice if you have a pattern of following and unfollowing people. They consider it a cheap method of gaining followers and attention for your profile.

• If you're following a ginormous number of people and only have a few followers yourself, it's usually a sign that you're trying to entice people to follow you but have provided very little value to the people who followed you in the first place. Twitter experts on the web seem to agree that it's safe to follow about four times the number of people following you, but no more.

• Here's a key big one—updates that consist of links, particularly sales links, more than they do conversation, or what Twitter calls "personal updates." Even as you're sharing things you need to be careful about the image you're presenting. Again, are you sharing, or are you force-distributing unwanted sales messages to a temporarily captive audience?

• Twitter also looks to see if a whole lot of people are blocking you. Note that you should be concerned way before Twitter is if you find this is the case—it means you're doing something wrong, offensive, or annoying. Since wrong, offensive, and annoying can only hurt your business you need to keep an eye on this number.

• Twitter looks to see if you are posting duplicate content over the course of multiple accounts, or multiple duplicate updates on one account. Post about that nifty new product once and only once. If you've done your job people will retweet it and it'll get to the other time zones that way. Don't hit Twitter with it again, and again, and again.

Twitter (A Little Birdie Told Me)

• This one's a biggie—remember #tags? If you try to use a #tag and then post a lot of unrelated stuff on it then you're running the risk of getting flagged as a spammer, even if what you say is innocent. Be relevant. A random statement is as odd and jarring on Twitter as it is at a real life party.

• Twitter also has issues with plagiarism—so make sure if you retweet you attribute the original user. While this doesn't fit with traditional visions of "spam" as e-mail spam defines it, it is a big Twitter no-no, akin to copying the answers off someone else's paper.

• Finally, there's one red flag that's beyond your control, somewhat—multiple spam complaints from users. It's out of your control, and then again it's not out of your control: users are not likely to report you as a spammer if you don't act like a spammer, and the ways to avoid that are clearly outlined for you.

Those are the only rules that are really counter-intuitive—the rest of Twitter's rules are common sense and amount to wiping your feet before coming into the house and keeping your mouth closed while you chew. However, there are a few more practices and rules you ought to take special note of.

• There's been a lot of buzz on the internet about selling Twitter accounts on Ebay or other venues in the hopes of raising some quick cash by cashing in on followers. This is against Twitter's terms of service unless you have a separate agreement with Twitter (there is no information on what would ever compel Twitter to create such an agreement). You are also not allowed to trade your account.

• You can't post any personal information. Why anyone would think is a good idea is beyond me, but go to e-mail or a web form if you want to take a credit card number for sales purposes. Twitter is too insecure even for a direct message transaction, even if it weren't against the terms and conditions.

• No links to porn or malware. Be careful what you link to, and if your business is of any kind of an adult nature make sure you present it as tastefully as possible—or consider other venues than Twitter to promote it.

Think Long Term

The fact that 60% of Twitter users quit in the first month is often used by Twitter naysayers as the defining statistic that "proves" there's not much worth to Twitter. These people of course ignore the millions of users who did stay. There are two reasons why people leave Twitter early on:

1) They didn't get it. This is very common, and "not getting it" is cited as the first stage of any Twitter user, whether they stay or not.

2) They thought they were going to see immediate results that they didn't see.

Twitter is not a short term gratification medium. It takes time to build followers. It takes time to build relation-ships. It will take time to see a pay-off. The pay-off will come, as numerous businesses large and small have demonstrated. The value is there, or those businesses would not continue to be there. You just can't rush in and hope to take the world by storm on the first day.

The hardest thing to master about Twitter is the value Twitter brings to listening, rather than to talking. It takes time to figure out when to listen and when to talk. In a way, the fact that you don't leap into twitter with 1,000 followers right away is a blessing. It gives you time to fumble around and make some mistakes before anyone is really looking. Sure, it's possible to call up every single tweet you've ever done over the life of your account. They are recorded, in perpetuity, forever and ever. Few people are going to bother to do this, however.

As you begin, don't obsess about sales and ROI—just jump in, try it, and see what Twitter can do. Allow yourself to be surprised and allow yourself to learn from others. It might not hurt to play around with a personal account before you get serious with your business account, but either way go in soft and let things unfold naturally. The value will begin presenting itself as you interact, and your best strategy will start to make sense to you the more you immerse yourself in the Twitter culture.

Be sure to avoid automated direct messages. Twitter users hate them, and they're counter-productive to building relationships. They broadcast that you are a blatant twitter marketer and not someone who actually cares about getting to know others—a reputation that can kill your effectiveness on Twitter.

Network and Meet Others

When you first get started, you might be tempted to follow people because you believe they are prospects or potential customers. This is of course a very valid function of Twitter and it's nothing you should ignore—but it's only half the equation.

You should try to follow people who you can learn from as well. Follow people who are interesting to you. Follow people you like listening to. Follow potential vendors and business partners who can solve some of your problems—allowing yourself to be helped and be a customer can not only show you how commerce works on Twitter, but it can also network and plug you into the community in a sincere way.

When it comes to Twitter that old phrase, "a rising tide lifts all boats," is true. The more you help others the more they're willing to turn around and help you. Yet again, even for a business account this is almost too opportunistic a description of Twitter. You're missing out if you're not using Twitter as an opportunity to get to know other people.

If you get to know a typical customer who never buys another thing from you, you've learned something. If you read a new blog post that teaches you to do business better because someone put it on a tweet, you and your business have benefitted from it. It's important to keep an open mind. Don't let your strategy tie you up to the point where you forget that you are essentially participating in a social exercise. Reach out to others, get your name out, but don't forget you're at a massive party.

This is where the brand thing gets fuzzy. You're doing brand management but you're also a human. Even if you're a human spokesperson for a larger company, ultimately you are still a human interacting with other humans. The moment you forget that you risk losing the brand battle you're working so hard to win in the first place.

Tossing Around Ideas

There are millions of other professionals on Twitter. Some of them are in your field—and some of them are not. Either sort of professional will have new ideas and new insights that you just don't have. Twitter can become a massive brainstorming session, opening you up to the perspectives and opinions of people who are outside of your company's four walls. All you have to do is initiate the conversation and find those professionals who will be willing to talk to you.

This is where you forget talking to "customers" and "prospects" for just a second and really zero in on the fact that you're in a forum where millions of 35-45 year old professionals, budding experts and voices in their field, join up to meet other people and talk about what has their attention. Some businesses pay thousands of dollars to have an independent consultant address this or that problem in the organization. On Twitter, you could have consultants weigh in for free—if you ask nicely enough.

Twitter is an open forum. CEOs are here—and they sometimes respond when addressed and spoken to in a relevant way. Marketing gurus, customer service geniuses—you name it, there is someone on Twitter who has insights. You might never be able to drop these people an e-mail or talk to them at a live party. You may not sit in the same class on the airplane. Yet on Twitter the playing field is even: if you're not boring and if you're not rude.

In some ways it's the sheer brevity of Twitter that makes this possible. A busy CEO doesn't necessarily have time for a long e-mail back to an unknown business person who addresses them with a question—but shooting an 140 character response, comment, or link doesn't take much time, particularly if said CEO was on the network to begin with. That same CEO is also networking and building relationships. The forum is appropriate.

Twitter Best Practices and Strategies

Yet it's not just the CEOs and big wigs you need to connect with—any professional with great ideas and a success story to share is someone you can learn from. Of course, you also have the ability to network by sharing your own expertise, a Twitter "best practice" if there ever was one.

You can use Twitter to put around joint ventures and projects around the world. Then you can use Twitter to bounce those ideas off of one another in real time. It's the ultimate brainstorming session with no limits. Once you've found the people who really have that sort of a mindset where they're open to working on ideas and happy to do so you've got a power in your pocket. You do this for the same reason you go to those networking groups and Chamber of Commerce meetings—to solidify your presence as a member of the business community, to make friends, to make yourself known, and to better your business.

Furthermore, there are a lot of creative new ways of doing business getting explored and implemented across the world today. It doesn't hurt to look into some of them, try to understand them, and ask questions. You might find an entire new way to supercharge your own performance— something that's vital as the economy grows ever more competitive.

Sneak Peeks and Backstage Passes

Though it may come as a surprise to you, people are often curious to know what's going on at a business. They want to know the parts they can't see. They're curious about what gets shoes onto shelves and radio shows onto the airwaves. Twitter provides an excellent opportunity for you to provide that "sneak peak".

Twitter (A Little Birdie Told Me)

This is why it is not inane to give status updates about your work day. A quick update that says, "Solving an operations issue today—permit fell through for new store," shows the hard work and difficulties a company can face just to get a new store open. This is also preventative PR. You're not making any excuses when the store doesn't open on time—but you've already let people know that there was an issue beyond your control.

Obviously there's some information about your business that's wholly proprietary and you don't want to share it. There are also some things that just aren't that fascinating —the sixth hundredth copy machine jam that day, for example, the meeting that bored everybody to tears, and ordering new legal pads among them. However the reasoning behind decisions, problems, solutions, and interesting parts of your business that people might not know about are an entirely different story.

Think of this exercise as offering those who follow you a "backstage pass" to the functions of your business. If you're a software developer, for example, you might give a sneak peek into the very frustrating process behind the never-ending stream of software updates and patches that every program seems to require these days. You'll not only provide information that people are curious but you'll perhaps stave off some of the irritation people feel when they have to download yet another patch or plug-in.

This of course does open you up to having people comment on how you're doing things—but that goes right back to trading ideas. If you're willing to set aside any defensiveness you may have about it, someone might just @reply or DM you a way they solved that very same problem. They might let you know a faster, cheaper, or less frustrating way to handle the problem. You never know.

Twitter Best Practices and Strategies

You're not just making yourself look human. You're not just networking. You're not just "keeping your name out there." You're telling a story about yourself, your company, your product, and your service. Keep the story interesting and you'll reap the maximum benefits from the telling.

Cross Promotion and Partnering

One of the fascinating things about any kind of internet marketing is the trend marketers have towards promoting other people's products and services. It's almost become more fashionable to step up and endorse someone else's work than it is to talk about your own. You gain respect by being important enough to offer an endorsement anybody will care about in the first place, and people get as curious about you as they were about the product you're endorsing, so this backwards way of thinking still benefits you.

There's also the factor of "joint venture marketing," which people who do business on the internet engage in regularly. This can range from ad swaps to giveaway events where digital products are offered in return for e-mail list membership. One of the very great dangers of doing joint venture marketing is that you might end up linking yourself up to someone who isn't quite worthy of you. Choose someone with a poor product or service and you may well end up painting yourself with the same brush, whether or not you otherwise deserve the negative reputation.

With Twitter you can test the waters a little bit. You can keep someone you've been thinking about approaching under consideration and watch how they handle themselves on Twitter. Twitter users have said that they believe the medium to be much more transparent because it's so off-the-cuff. With so little space to use people sometimes put

less thought into what they're saying. They build a reputation and they show off who they are, sometimes without
fully meaning to.

Once you've gained a positive impression of someone,
Twitter makes it easy to contact them and begin pitching
the joint ventures in a way that doesn't waste anybody's
time. After this initial interest has been established you
and your budding business partner can launch a more in-
depth discussion over e-mail, true IM, or the telephone.

You don't, however, have to wait until you have created a
formal partnership to endorse someone else's work.
Tweeting other people's blog posts, after all, is a way of endorsing the author of those blogs. Tweeting a news item
about another company is a way of promoting that company (so be careful what you say, if anything, about the competition. It may just work in their favor instead of in
yours).

Embrace Real Time Broadcasting

Properly #tagged real-time broadcasts of interesting things
are winners. Often this is talked about in the context of
seminars and trade shows, but really, you can real-time
broadcast about anything. If you're out at an interesting
hot air balloon race you can broadcast that, if you feel it fits
with your personal brand and Twitter mission.

Think about it: live television news feeds have always been
considered more valuable than pre-recorded ones. That's
what makes a live real time broadcasting feed from Twitter
all the more exciting. You're there, things are happening,
and you're taking the time to share it with others who
might be interested in knowing more. People are free to

skim right past if they're not interested in particular—that's one reason you #tag it.

Remember, too, that you can create your own seminars and real-time broadcast them, answering questions as they come in. This is a fantastic way to build value and an audience. This is also a fantastic way to interact with people who have already shown an interest in who you are and what you do by stopping to attend.

Stay on Top of the Game

Twitter is getting so much attention that it evolves daily. The etiquette evolves. The applications you can marry to Twitter evolves. The company itself is evolving, as it attempts to understand how it might monetize itself and what kind of business model will suit it best.

A dedicated Twitter marketer's best friend is to stay on top of these trends. There are some people who dismiss Twitter as a passing fad—but it isn't. Twitter is here to stay, much as blogs are (remember that blogs were dismissed as a passing fad as well). Things will grow and change. New features and protocols will become available.

Right now, your customers are on Twitter, and that's why you should be too. As more and more people embrace Twitter the demographics of those customers who interact with you on social media will change—which may mean changes in your strategy or approach. It may mean opening up a second Twitter account to address a different function of your business. You should keep abreast of what's going on and evaluate your strategy each and every year. When the next hot internet trend hits, you'll read about it in 140 characters (or less).

Also available from
The Butler Publishing Group

ISBN-10: 1442164549
ISBN-13: 9781442164543

Available on Amazon.com -
http://tinyurl.com/qk6z7b

www.ingramcontent.com/pod-product-compliance
Lightning Source LLC
Chambersburg PA
CBHW071303170526
45165CB00003B/1401